Illustrator:
Bruce Hedges

Editor:
Mary Kaye Taggart

Editorial Project Manager:
Karen J. Goldfluss, M.S. Ed.

Editor in Chief:
Sharon Coan, M.S. Ed.

Art Director:
Elayne Roberts

Associate Designer:
Denise Bauer

Cover Artist:
Chris Macabitas

Product Manager:
Phil Garcia

Imaging:
James Edward Grace

Publishers:
Rachelle Cracchiolo, M.S. Ed.
Mary Dupuy Smith, M.S. Ed.

How to Prepare Your Students for
Standardized Tests

Primary

Author:

Julia Jasmine, M.A.

Teacher Created Materials, Inc.
6421 Industry Way
Westminster, CA 92683
www.teachercreated.com
ISBN 1-57690-130-0
©1997 Teacher Created Materials, Inc.
Revised, 1999
Made in U.S.A.

Table of Contents